Published by SL Resources, Inc.
A Division of Student Life

© 2010 SL Resources, Inc.

All rights reserved. No part of this publication may be reproduced, stored in a retrieval system, or transmitted in any form or by any means, electronic, mechanical, photocopying, recording, or otherwise, without the prior written permission of Student Life Resources, Inc. Address all correspondence to:

Student Life
Attn: Ministry Resources
2183 Parkway Lake Drive
Birmingham, AL 35226

Unless otherwise indicated, all Scripture quotations are taken from the Holy Bible: New International Version (North American Edition), copyright ©1973, 1978, 1984, by International Bible Society. Used by permission of Zondervan Publishing House.

ISBN-10: 1935040812
ISBN-13: 9781935040811

31 Verses Every Teenager Should Know™

www.studentlife.com
www.31verses.com

Printed in the United States of America

TABLE OF CONTENTS

Introduction — i
How To Use — ii

THE PEOPLE OF GOD
What did God's people look like in the Old Testament?

Verse 1: Genesis 12:2 — 1
Verse 2: Exodus 19:5 — 3
Verse 3: Leviticus 26:12 — 5
Verse 4: Zechariah 8:22 — 7
Verse 5: Psalm 98:2 — 9
Verse 6: Hebrews 9:26b — 11

THE GLOBAL CHURCH
Who is the Church?

Verse 7: 1 Corinthians 1:2 — 13
Verse 8: Colossians 3:11 — 15
Verse 9: Acts 1:8 — 17
Verse 10: Matthew 16:16 — 19
Verse 11: John 16:7 — 21
Verse 12: Ephesians 1:13 — 23
Verse 13: 1 Timothy 3:15 — 25
Verse 14: Philippians 1:29 — 27
Verse 15: Revelation 21:3 — 29
Verse 16: Ephesians 5:23 — 31
Verse 17: 1 Corinthians 12:27 — 33

THE LOCAL BODY

What does the Church look like in a local community?

- Verse 18: Romans 12:5 — 35
- Verse 19: Romans 10:14 — 37
- Verse 20: Acts 13:2 — 39
- Verse 21: James 1:27 — 41
- Verse 22: Philippians 2:15 — 43

How does the local community interact with unbelievers?

- Verse 23: John 13:35 — 45
- Verse 24: Acts 4:34-35 — 47
- Verse 25: Ephesians 4:11-12 — 49
- Verse 26: 2 Timothy 2:2 — 51
- Verse 27: Acts 17:11 — 53
- Verse 28: Matthew 18:15 — 55
- Verse 29: James 5:16 — 57
- Verse 30: Galatians 6:1 — 59
- Verse 31: Hebrews 10:25 — 61

Closing — 64
About the Author — 66

INTRO

Church. Does this word remind you of a building or location? Does it remind you of a service where people meet together? What if I substituted the phrase *the people of God* for the word *church*? How would your perception change?

The word used for church in the New Testament actually means "the ones who are called out." God has called out His people for His purpose—and these people are His Church in the world. They're His reflection and His representatives in the world. This is what Church is about. This is who the Church is.

You will see throughout this book (and even on this page) that sometimes the *c* is capitalized, as in *Church*, and sometimes it's not, as in *church*. The big *c* Church is a way to talk about God's people across the entire globe. The little *c* church is a way to talk about the local community of God's people. This book is here to help you understand both and how you fit into each of them. God's people aren't just the nation of Israel from the Old Testament, and the church isn't a building on your local street. You are the Church. You are a part of God's chosen people to represent Him to the world.

Our culture often tells us that religion is irrelevant and dying. Perhaps religion is empty to some. Maybe this tainted view of religion has caused some people to view God as insignificant. But when the Church is active and alive and being God's hands and feet in the world, our culture sees Him for who He is. That's why the Church is important. That's why we must know who He has called us to be as His people, His Church.

His hands and feet,

Jenny Riddle
Editor

how to use

Now that you own this incredible little book, you may be wondering, "What do I do with it?"

Glad you asked. The great thing about this book is that you can use it just about any way you want.

It's not a system. It's a resource that can be used in ways that are as unique and varied as you are.

A few suggestions:

THE ONE-MONTH PLAN
On this plan, you'll read one devotion each day for a month. This is a great way to immerse yourself in the Bible for a month-long period. (OK, we realize that every month doesn't have 31 days. But 28 or 30 is close enough to 31, right?) The idea is to cover a lot of information in a short amount of time.

THE SCRIPTURE MEMORY PLAN
The idea behind this plan is to memorize the verse for each day's devotion; you don't move on to the next devotion until you've memorized the Scripture you're on. If you're like most people, this might take you more than one day per devotion. So this plan takes a slower approach.

THE "I'M NO WILLIAM SHAKESPEARE" PLAN
Don't like to write or journal? This plan is for you. . . . Listen, not everyone expresses themselves the same way. If you don't like to express yourself through writing, that's OK. Simply read the devotion for each verse, then read the questions. Think about them. Pray through them. But don't feel as if you have to journal if you don't want to.

THE STRENGTH IN NUMBERS PLAN
God designed humans for interaction. We're social creatures. How cool would it be if you could go through *31: Community* with your friends? Get a group of friends together. Consider agreeing to read five verses each week then meeting to talk about them.

Pretty simple, huh? Choose a plan. Or make up your own. But get started already. What are you waiting for?

ii

VERSE 1

> I WILL MAKE YOU INTO A GREAT NATION AND
> I WILL BLESS YOU; I WILL MAKE YOUR NAME
> GREAT, AND YOU WILL BE A BLESSING.
>
> GENESIS 12:2

Have you ever met a one-upper? You know, that guy who always has to tell a story that makes your fantastic story seem like nothing. I usually try avoidance tactics with people like that. But in this case, he's unavoidable. Abraham, I mean. I can just see us sitting in a room, chatting it up, and I say, "Remember that time I was promised a car for graduation? I got an amazing Volkswagen—exactly what I wanted." Then he replies, "Yeah, I remember that time I got something I was promised. The whole world was blessed through me." OK, Abraham. You win.

Read Genesis 12:1-3. God made some seriously big promises to Abraham in this passage. He promised Abraham that he would be the beginning of God's chosen nation. That was huge, especially for a man who, up to that point, didn't even have children. Then, God promised Abraham that through that chosen nation, He would bless the entire world. That was even bigger than being the beginning of a nation, my friends. It was much, much bigger. God was saying that through the line of Abraham, the ultimate blessing would come to humankind in Jesus Christ. Because Abraham was obedient to God's call to leave his homeland and walk by faith in what God called him to do, God birthed a nation through him. Jesus Christ was born through the line of Abraham's descendents.

And now because of Christ, we all belong to this same great family. We're part of the biggest family in existence with the greatest message the world has ever heard. All of this happened because of a promise God made to a man named Abraham. Nobody's going to one-up that.

REFLECT

1. What can you learn about God through His promises to Abraham?

2. Why are God's promises to Abraham important to you?

3. How does the truth that we're all a part of a family affect your interaction with other believers?

VERSE 2

Now if you obey me fully and keep my covenant, then out of all nations you will be my treasured possession. Although the whole earth is mine . . .
EXODUS 19:5

Pretty much everybody wants to be unique in one way or another. Some people go to great lengths to be dramatically unique—such as the guy in the mall who has metal spikes sticking out of his shaved head or the girl at the park who never wears shoes and writes poetic phrases on her feet. These people appear different. They draw attention to themselves because they don't look or act like everyone else. As a child of God, not only is looking different a possibility, it's a requirement. It always has been.

Read Exodus 19:3-6. God had some things to tell His chosen people through Moses. He wanted them to know that they could trust Him. He sent a spokesperson on their behalf to ensure their freedom from slavery. He parted waters for them and defeated armies for them. They were His treasured possession. God was now telling them how they should live as His children. They were to be holy—to be set apart—by obeying God's commandments. By doing this, the other nations would look at them and see that God's people were different. God wanted Israel to look different from those around them so that they could be a representation of God's holiness to the entire world. Their obedience was a testimony to all who were on the outside looking in.

Just as Israel's did, our lives must look different so that we will be a testimony to others about God. If you want to be different, don't do it to draw attention to yourself; make sure that your difference draws attention to the God you serve so that others might know Him.

REFLECT

1. What is at stake by the way that you live as a Christ-follower?

2. Do you typically want to blend in with others or to be completely different? Why is living differently from others often difficult for us?

3. In what ways does your life not reflect God's holiness?

VERSE
three

I WILL WALK AMONG YOU AND BE YOUR GOD,
AND YOU WILL BE MY PEOPLE.

LEVITICUS 26:12

If a city wants to host the Olympic Games, its representatives must begin the bidding process nine years before the games actually take place. Two years after the bidding process begins, the International Olympic Committee (IOC) votes to select one of the candidate cities as the host city for the Games (which will take place in another seven years). When the IOC announces the host city, anyone with access to a TV or the Internet watches, or at least checks in occasionally, to see which of the candidate cities became the chosen one—the city selected to have the sights, sounds, tourists, athletes, and media blitz of the Olympics dwell with them for a time.

Read Leviticus 26:11-12. In this passage, God told His people that His desire was to be with them. His presence would dwell with Israel, and He would walk among them and attach His name to them. At this time in the life of God's people, His presence would dwell with them in the Ark of the Covenant within their Tabernacle. They didn't have to send in bids for Him to come, but He did require their obedience. They were His chosen people, and He wanted to dwell with them because they were His. He didn't relate to them from a distance. He was personal.

We're all human, and we all mess up. But think about this amazing truth: God, the Creator of the entire universe, doesn't just know you from a distance—He's personal. No matter what we do, we're not good enough to deserve a relationship with Him. But no matter what we do, He's faithful. We can take heart that, unlike cities vying to host the Olympics, we don't have to send out bids for God to choose us. As Christ-followers, we're chosen by God. And, unlike the Olympics when the games are over, He never leaves the ones He has chosen.

REFLECT

1. How can you have a personal relationship with God and maintain a reverence for Him at the same time?

2. How does God feel distant to you at times?

3. How does it affect you to know the truth that He's always present with His children?

VERSE 4

And many peoples and powerful nations will come to Jerusalem to seek the LORD Almighty and entreat him.
ZECHARIAH 8:22

My mom has always been amazing. When I was growing up, she would bedazzle the outside of my lunch bag and put a note inside that said, "I love you this much." (If you've missed out on the joys of a BeDazzler check out www.mybedazzler.com, and imagine how dazzling your world can be.) Beside those words would be a drawing of a person with arms so long that they stretched onto the back of the page. The drawing was passed around the lunch table every day. My friends always ran to hug my mom whenever they saw her because they knew anybody who took the time to make that kind of lunch bag for her daughter had to be awesome.

Read Zechariah 8:20-23. In chapter 8, Zechariah told Israel that although they were experiencing trials because of their disobedience, God was going to restore them. He was restoring His Temple, and He was going to turn their fasting into feasting. He was going to be faithful to His people even though they'd been unfaithful to Him. People outside of the nation of Israel would see how God dealt with His children—that He was holy and merciful. His fame would spread throughout the land. The nations would come to seek God because of the things they'd seen and heard in Israel, His chosen people.

You and I are similar to Israel in this passage. We have all been disobedient to God in our sin, and although we're unfaithful, He's faithful to us. He shows His amazing love for us by His grace and forgiveness. When He does this, we can proclaim and reflect His character to others. So, even though you haven't been given a bedazzled lunch bag, pray that the people around you will come to know Him by the way He has faithfully and lovingly transformed you.

REFLECT

1. How does the Book of Zechariah say that other nations were going to respond to what they saw God doing for His people?

2. How can people see God's love and faithfulness when they look at your life?

3. How can you view all of your situations as opportunities to reflect God's grace to others?

VERSE 5

THE LORD MADE HIS SALVATION KNOWN AND REVEALED HIS RIGHTEOUSNESS TO THE NATIONS.

PSALM 98:2

I once was an OREO for a day. A huge, inflatable suit was involved as well as constant waving and handing out cookies. Before I was allowed to stand outside the grocery store to do my job, though, I had to listen to an intense speech about how I was a representation of the cookie and the company. If people were going to see the value and the goodness in the OREO that day, it was going to be through me. In a way, the children of Israel got to experience what it was like to be an inflatable OREO.

Read Psalm 98:2-3. The writer of this psalm was reminding the people of Israel of what God had done. He had delivered them, provided for their needs, and been steadfast in His love. He had made His salvation known to them, but it didn't stop there. God's salvation wasn't just for the people of Israel; it was for the world. The whole earth was watching what God had done for His people. The psalmist said that during the time of the Old Testament, God's interaction with Israel was His way of showing salvation to all nations.

You and I share in the implications of this psalm, too. Through our lives, God shows the world how He loves, redeems, and transforms. What God has done for you and me through our salvation is a witness to everyone around us. Wonderful were the ways that He worked in the lives of the children of Israel, and wonderful are the ways He continually shows His love through you and me. We, as believers, are God's representatives—kind of like His OREOS.

REFLECT

1. What was one way the nations outside of Israel could see and know about God?

2. If you are truly God's representative, why are your decisions and actions so important?

3. How can God use you to show Himself and His salvation to others?

VERSE 6

But now he has appeared once for all at the end of the ages to do away with sin by the sacrifice of himself.
HEBREWS 9:26B

Do you think about Alexander Graham Bell every time you have a phone conversation or send a text? Probably not. You should, though, because if he hadn't invented the telephone, things would be very different. We should thank him now that we can communicate without having to write letters or walk long distances just to talk to each other. He forever changed the way we relate to others.

Read Hebrews 9:24-28. So far, we've read about how God chose the nation of Israel to be His special people. He told them to walk with Him by living according to His covenant, which required animal sacrifices to atone for the Israelites' sins. These sacrifices provided a way for them to have a relationship with God. Then Jesus came and was the ultimate sacrifice for all people for all time. Christ's sacrifice made a new covenant available to the whole world. All of His followers, regardless of nationality, are His chosen people. All of His followers are the people of God.

God's promise to bless the world through Abraham is now a reality through Christ. As Christ's followers, we receive that promised blessing when we place our faith in Him. Jesus has done everything that's necessary for the salvation of every person, and now all people can have access to the Father through a relationship with Christ. It doesn't take animal sacrifices or a prophetic voice to relate to God anymore. Even more than the phone changed the way that we communicate, Christ's sacrifice forever changed the way that we relate to God. Think about this—we're His chosen people, His nation of priests, not because of the nation we were born in but because He sacrificed Himself for us. We're the people of God!

REFLECT

1. Why don't you as a Christ-follower have to provide sacrifices for your sins anymore?

2. Have you ever thought of yourself as part of God's chosen people? How does this truth affect how you see your purpose as a Christ-follower?

3. Write a prayer thanking God for what He has done for you through Christ.

VERSE
seven

TO THE CHURCH OF GOD IN CORINTH, TO THOSE SANCTIFIED IN CHRIST JESUS AND CALLED TO BE HOLY, TOGETHER WITH ALL THOSE EVERYWHERE WHO CALL ON THE NAME OF OUR LORD JESUS CHRIST—THEIR LORD AND OURS . . .
1 CORINTHIANS 1:2

Time to test your world geography skills. I know you've got them, so don't be shaking your head like you don't. Where is Tonga located? Any guesses? OK, I'll tell you. It's a group of 171 islands in the South Pacific. In 2002, a church in Nuku'alofa, Tonga started constructing their first church building, and they enjoyed their first service there in 2009. So why should you care about people that you didn't even know existed until about three sentences ago? Well, my friend, you should care because they're your family.

Read 1 Corinthians 1:2. In this letter, Paul addressed some key issues that the church at Corinth faced. One issue within their church was unity. So right out of the gate, Paul made it very clear that they served the same God and trusted in the same Jesus Christ for salvation as every other man and woman that called on Him. Though God chose to bring salvation through one nation, He is calling the whole world to Himself. The new covenant that Jesus brought made every Christ-follower a part of the same family.

Paul's message for the Corinthian church is His message to us as well. We're not only part of a local body of believers through our churches, but we're a part of the biggest family in the world. Our God is also the God of our brothers and sisters in Canada, Brazil, Uganda, China and places we may not even know about—such as Tonga. We're all in the family, and we're all one in Christ. Isn't it exciting that we have such a wide variety of brothers and sisters all over the world?

REFLECT

1. Why is unity an important attitude for believers to have?

2. How does this truth change your view of God's Church?

3. How can you be involved in supporting your brothers and sisters around the world?

VERSE 8

Here there is no Greek or Jew, circumcised or uncircumcised, barbarian, Scythian, slave or free, but Christ is all, and is in all. COLOSSIANS 3:11

"People say that it can't work, black and white; well, here we make it work, every day." *Remember the Titans* is a movie based on true events that took place in a small town in Virginia in 1971. The Titans high school football team was forced to integrate races that year. The players, who may have normally hated each other because of their prejudices, came together to play football and bonded as brothers when they realized that their divisions were phony and hurtful to everyone.

Read Colossians 3:11. The church at Colossae faced what every culture in history has faced. Everyone had an ingrained desire to be better than those around them. So they used their religion, their social status, their education, and their family history to make themselves feel more important and more worthy. When they became followers of Christ, this was a hard habit to break, and Paul noticed how it interfered with their godly views of each other. So he reminded them that no Christ-follower has an advantage over another. He said they are one in Christ, and in His eyes all people are equal.

That message remains the same for us today. Our culture likes to put us into groups, whether racially, politically, denominationally, educationally, or otherwise. As believers, though, we must remember that the gospel is available to all people, and the Church is composed of all believers. We're all unworthy people who are loved undeservedly. We all operate under the same grace that Christ freely gives. We serve a God who shows no discrimination, and we bear His image. People say it can't work, being unified with people so different than we are, but here each of us must make it work, every day.

REFLECT

1. What kinds of people do you have prejudices against? Why?

2. How do the unity of the church and the spread of the gospel demand that you not hold prejudices against any person?

3. What will you do to ensure that you see everyone around you as equal in Christ?

VERSE 9

> BUT YOU WILL RECEIVE POWER WHEN THE HOLY SPIRIT COMES ON YOU; AND YOU WILL BE MY WITNESSES IN JERUSALEM, AND IN ALL JUDEA AND SAMARIA, AND TO THE ENDS OF THE EARTH.
>
> ACTS 1:8

Big Foot and the Loch Ness Monster have devoted fans that spend much of their existence trying to get one good, convincing picture of the mysterious creatures so that the world can believe they exist. Let's be honest; many people aren't buying the hype. It may be due to the fact that these "witnesses" often present themselves in an unreliable way, particularly by having little, if any, indisputable evidence. Did you know that if you're a follower of Christ, you're called to be a reliable and faithful witness to something that not everyone believes?

Read Acts 1:8. Jesus chose His followers to continue His mission in the world. Christ commanded them to be witnesses by giving testimony of Him to the entire world. The disciples were not to accomplish this task on their own, though. Jesus was going to send the Holy Spirit to them so that they would live through His power. The Holy Spirit would help the disciples carry out Christ's mission because they couldn't do it in their own abilities. The pictures of their lives and the words of their mouths would be testimonies for all to see and hear. In the same way, the Church's purpose is to be witnesses of God to all peoples. This mission is so important that God Himself empowers His people to do it.

We've been called to be witnesses to what God has done and is still doing at home and around the world. People all around the world are looking to see if God is real and if He loves them. We have proof by the way that our lives have been transformed by the Holy Spirit into the image of Christ. We're living examples of Christ, and He calls us to the purpose of making Him known to the world.

REFLECT

1. In what ways can you be a witness for Christ in your home? At school or on sports teams? To the world?

2. How does your responsibility to be a witness for Christ affect the decisions that you make?

3. Write down a few people that you know need to see your witness about Jesus.

VERSE 10

Simon Peter answered, "You are the Christ, the Son of the living God." MATTHEW 16:16

Many people believe facts about Jesus, but not everyone puts their faith in Him. Some religions believe that Jesus was just a good man or a good teacher. C.S. Lewis, the author of the *Chronicles of Narnia*, wrote, "Either this man was, and is, the Son of God: or else a madman or something worse. You can shut Him up for a fool, you can spit at Him and kill Him as a demon; or you can fall at His feet and call Him Lord and God. But let us not come with any patronizing nonsense about His being a great human teacher. He has not left that open to us. He did not intend to."[1]

Read Matthew 16:13-18. Israel had heard the prophecy that God would send a great prophet to His people. Using this frame of reference, the people speculated that Jesus was a good spiritual teacher, in line with the great prophets. Jesus asked His disciples who they thought He was. Peter spoke up and identified Him as "the Christ, the Son of the living God." He was saying that Jesus wasn't merely a good teacher; Jesus was actually the Son of God in human flesh—the key to the disciples' faith. There was no relationship with God without Him. Jesus said His Church would be built upon a people who understood this truth.

So who is Jesus Christ to Christ-followers? If He's not the Son of the living God, if He didn't save us from our sins through His death and resurrection, then we're wasting our lives following a crazy person. Fortunately, we can trust that Jesus is who He says He is. This faith in Christ binds us together and drives our mission to tell the world the good news. There's no way to the Father but through Jesus, and there's no Church without the foundation of Christ.

REFLECT

1. How does your understanding of Jesus as the foundation of the Church change how you think about how all churches across the globe are connected?

2. Why is it important that you fully believe in the true identity of Jesus as the Son of God, the Messiah?

3. How can you make Jesus the foundation of your life? How can you help point to Him as the foundation of your youth group?

¹Lewis, C.S. *Mere Christianity*. New York, N.Y.: Macmillan Publishing Company, 1996. Pg. 56.

VERSE
eleven

> BUT I TELL YOU THE TRUTH: IT IS FOR YOUR GOOD THAT I AM GOING AWAY. UNLESS I GO AWAY, THE COUNSELOR WILL NOT COME TO YOU; BUT IF I GO, I WILL SEND HIM TO YOU.
>
> JOHN 16:7

Modern technology is amazing! We have planes that can fly themselves! Sometimes, the U.S. military uses planes that are flown remotely or by a preset flight plan. Referred to as drones, they don't need a pilot to fly. But in spite of all our technological gadgetry, there are still limitations. From cars to trains to drones, all of our vehicles need someone to operate them or tell them where to go. They cannot do their jobs apart from the ability and power of their operators.

Read John 16:5-11. The time had come for Jesus to experience the suffering of the cross and physically leave His disciples. He explained that He would not leave them alone but would send them His Spirit. Jesus said that they would be better off when He was gone because the Holy Spirit would be present with them. While on earth, Jesus was only in one place at a time. The Holy Spirit, though, would be present with all believers (His Church) at all times all over the world. He would guide them to carry out God's mission. Only God could accomplish His work, so He sent His Spirit to empower His Church.

No matter how much we think we can live in our own power, we're similar to drones: we can't really do anything on our own. We can't call the shots or make things happen with our own power or direction. God has commanded us to do some pretty amazing things, but without Him, we're useless. Maybe some of us have never looked for direction from the Holy Spirit, or maybe we're just ignoring it. Whatever the case may be, we have a job to do and it's time for us to ask the Holy Spirit to take control and direct our lives.

REFLECT

1. Do you ever feel overwhelmed in trying to live a godly life? According to this passage, what's the only way that you can live according to God's calling?

2. What's something that you feel unequipped to do, that you need to ask the Holy Spirit to do through you?

3. Write a prayer asking the Holy Spirit to control and lead your life.

VERSE 12

And you also were included in Christ when you heard the word of truth, the gospel of your salvation. Having believed, you were marked in him with a seal, the promised Holy Spirit.
EPHESIANS 1:13

I'm obsessed with the Olympics. When I was young I wanted to be an athlete who carried my country's flag in the opening ceremony. It's amazing to me how many times I've heard athletes say that they were honored to have been a part of the games and wear their nation's colors and symbols. As representatives of their countries, they take pride in being marked for their nations and want the world to know it. As representatives of God's Kingdom, we're marked by our Heavenly Father so the entire world can know it.

Read Ephesians 1:13-14. In ancient times, often a king would wear a signet ring that had his royal seal on it. Whenever official correspondence was sent out from the palace, the letter would be sealed with hot wax and the king would put the imprint of his ring in the seal. There was no doubt whom the letter was from, because the seal was one of a kind. Paul used that imagery in this passage to say that God puts His seal on believers' lives when He gives them the Holy Spirit. God's very presence dwells within His people. His presence empowers and guides His people to live according to His calling and to take His presence to the world.

There should be no doubt to whom we belong because we bear the royal seal of God. We will represent the King to the world. When you and I became believers in Jesus Christ, we were marked with the Holy Spirit. This truth means we're never too young and never too inexperienced to make a difference for Christ. We're His Church, His people, and we can go into the world with full confidence in His ability in our lives.

REFLECT

1. How can you, as a believer, take God's presence to the world?

2. How does your role as a representative of God to the world affect how you interact with others? With your family? With unbelievers?

3. Thank God for sealing you with His Holy Spirit and ask that same Spirit to fill you and equip you for the day.

VERSE 13

IF I AM DELAYED, YOU WILL KNOW HOW PEOPLE OUGHT TO CONDUCT THEMSELVES IN GOD'S HOUSEHOLD, WHICH IS THE CHURCH OF THE LIVING GOD, THE PILLAR AND FOUNDATION OF THE TRUTH.

1 TIMOTHY 3:15

The end of World War II was marked by Japan's final surrender to the Allied nations. The formal signing of Japan's surrender took place in a celebrated ceremony aboard the *U.S.S. Missouri* in Tokyo Bay. Representatives from the Allied nations and Japan were on board the ship to sign the surrender documents. Emperor Hirohito of Japan was not on board. Neither was Harry Truman, the President of the United States. Neither was Winston Churchill, the Prime Minister of England. So, who signed these globe-impacting documents? Their national representatives did! These men carried the message of peace and the authority of truth given to them by their nations.

Read 1 Timothy 3:15. Paul told Timothy how the Church is to function so that the world would look at it and see the truth of the gospel. The Church is God's representative to the world. When His people live and work together in the way that God commanded, the world is able to see the truth. The Church is the very foundation and center of truth in the world. It carries and reflects the Spirit of God wherever its members are, and that Spirit speaks of the one who is truth: Jesus Christ.

Our world is desperate for truth. As they look at the Body of Christ they should be able to get the answer they've been looking for their entire lives. As God's representatives in the world, we must allow God to transform our lives so that we're living examples of His character. When we go into our schools, malls, city, nation, and world, we're living out a picture of God. We're to live so that the world gets a clear picture of who He really is.

REFLECT

1. How are you a part of God's mission? How are you taking and representing truth to the world around you?

2. How are you helping your local church represent the truth of Jesus Christ to the world?

3. Thank Jesus for being the truth. Think of at least one way to get involved with the followers of Christ around you to proclaim His truth today, and write it down.

VERSE 14

For it has been granted to you on behalf of Christ not only to believe on him, but also to suffer for him.
PHILIPPIANS 1:29

Working out isn't really my idea of fun. When my friend begged me to join her for a spinning class at the gym, I reluctantly agreed. She assured me that it would feel like a leisurely 30-minute bike ride that would go by quickly with the help of a good iPod playlist. I lasted three weeks. It was actually a 45-minute class in a small, dark room. I definitely couldn't hear my music over the drill sergeant, who was under the impression that I should be on the brink of death by the end of the class. If I'd only known what I was getting myself into . . .

Read Philippians 1:27-30. Paul wrote the Book of Philippians while he was in jail for preaching the gospel. He encouraged the church at Philippi because they were also encountering trials and persecution. Life as a Christ-follower was not one of comfort or safety for these first-century Christians. Paul knew that living as a Christ-follower meant encountering opposition and enduring persecution. God's people would suffer, but Paul encouraged them not only to remain firm in their faith but also to consider suffering for Christ a privilege. When God's people suffer for His sake, they identify with Christ.

Following Christ is hard. We like to talk about amazing grace, a loving God, and a redeeming Savior. All of that's true, but it's not a complete picture of daily living. The hard part is living a life so transformed by Jesus that those who hate Christ will want us to suffer. Being a Christ-follower is about grace, love, joy and peace, but it's also about suffering. Getting in shape isn't intended to be easy. Neither is following Christ. Do you know what you're getting yourself into?

REFLECT

1. If Christ suffered for the gospel, why do you think that His Church would avoid it? Why is persecution a testimony of your faith in Christ?

2. What were your expectations for following Christ? Did you expect difficult times to come because of your faith?

3. How does being a part of a body of believers encourage you to live for Christ even when it's hard?

VERSE
fifteen

AND I HEARD A LOUD VOICE FROM THE THRONE SAYING, "NOW THE DWELLING OF GOD IS WITH MEN, AND HE WILL LIVE WITH THEM. THEY WILL BE HIS PEOPLE, AND GOD HIMSELF WILL BE WITH THEM AND BE THEIR GOD."

REVELATION 21:3

Trail mix and I have a love/hate relationship. For the most part it's salty and sweet goodness, but inevitably there's one kind of nut or dried fruit that I really don't like. So I pick through the bag and end up with a pile of one certain thing that I eventually feed to the dog or throw away. It would be so nice if the trail mix were full of only the things that I love most!

Read Revelation 21:1-4. John wrote this book while isolated on an island called Patmos. He had been exiled there as a result of persecution. Jesus revealed His future plan for creation through visions to John so he could share it with the Church. In this passage, John described a voice from heaven that declared that one day, this earth would pass away and God's people would dwell with Him for eternity in a perfect relationship. God's Church is eternal. Even though it faces persecution and suffering, the Church's certain future is eternity with God. The future will be a perfect one with no pain, suffering, death, or tears. Don't you know how excited John was when he heard this, considering his circumstances!

Though we have the presence of God dwelling in us, we're still living in a world that's imperfect. There's good mixed in with the bad. We still encounter physical death. There's still disease. Persecution and suffering exist all over the world. Brothers and sisters, what good news it is to read this revelation that John received from Christ. It will not always be this way! One day we'll dwell in a physical place of perfection with our King Jesus. We won't have to look through a mixed bag to pick out the good stuff. Everything will be perfect.

REFLECT

1. How can the Church find hope in this passage?

2. How can the certainty of your future encourage you in the current, sin-filled world?

3. How do these truths change the way you look at things that make it hard to live in this world?

VERSE 16

For the husband is the head of the wife as Christ is the head of the church, his body, of which he is the Savior.
EPHESIANS 5:23

"You're not the boss of me." Have you ever heard or spoken those words? My childhood was marked with that phrase because I had two older sisters who were certain that their purpose in life was to order me around. If we're completely honest, most of us struggle when our parents, teachers, coaches, or friends try to tell us what to do. Submission is just not always easy.

Read Ephesians 5:23-27. Paul wrote these words to the church at Ephesus to help them understand that the Church is under the leadership and authority of Christ. The Church doesn't act according to its own mission or beliefs. The Church looks to Jesus as its head and submits to His authority and mission. Christ showed His love for His Church through His sacrifice on the cross. Because of this love, He made a way for His Church to become more and more like Him so that it reflects His holiness.

Many people think that they can follow Christ according to their own standards—that they can live as if He's not the boss. However, just as Christ is the head of His Church, He's also the head of you and me. We must submit our lives to His authority and align our lives with His mission because we no longer belong to ourselves: Jesus has purchased us with His sacrifice. As we submit to His commands and purpose for our lives, He will purify us and make us more like Him. We'll be transformed by laying our lives at His feet and saying, "Jesus, I trust your leadership and submit to your ways." What a beautiful picture to see the Church—the people of God—saying, "Jesus is the boss of me."

REFLECT

1. Why is submitting to the leadership of someone else difficult?

2. How are you supposed to respond to the headship of Jesus in your life?

3. What areas of your life do you need to submit to Christ today? Take time to confess those things, and ask the Holy Spirit to transform your heart as you surrender your life to Jesus.

VERSE 17

> NOW YOU ARE THE BODY OF CHRIST, AND EACH ONE OF YOU IS A PART OF IT.
> 1 CORINTHIANS 12:27

Miss Patty was my music teacher. I will forever associate her name with the crushing of dreams. One day I confided in her that I wanted to pursue musical theater. You know, Broadway and big lights kind of stuff. She gently let me know that my voice wasn't really Broadway material. She suggested that, because I loved theater so much, I could take a different role such as set design or stage management. "How lame," I thought. "I don't want a second-hand role." Do you ever feel that way in church? I mean, not everybody can be a popular worship leader or pastor, right?

Read 1 Corinthians 12:4-27. Paul explained to the Corinthian church that the Church is Christ's body—His hands and feet to the world. Paul stated that every believer was gifted by the Holy Spirit for the purpose of building up the Body of Christ and fulfilling His purpose. In the Corinthian church, some of these gifts were considered better than others. Paul clearly told them that one gift was not more important than any other, and they all were for the benefit of the whole Body of Christ—the Church. Representing Christ in a very real way means that every member of the Church is vital to His mission. There are no second-hand gifts.

The same is true of us as believers in the Church. All of us are a part of the Body of Christ, and God has gifted each of us so that we can be a special part of His mission. There are no second-hand roles, and God doesn't overlook anyone. Everyone has a place, everyone plays a part, and every part is important. A teenager has just as important a role in God's work through the Church as a worship leader. So what are you waiting for? Get to it, my friend.

REFLECT

1. Why do you consider some roles in the Church to be more important than others?

2. Why is it important to see that we all play a role in the Church?

3. Take some time to think about the talents and abilities that God has given you and how you can use them to benefit the Body of Christ. Write down some places in the church where you can serve as the Body of Christ.

VERSE 18

So in Christ we who are many form one body, and each member belongs to all the others. ROMANS 12:5

Sitting in Biology class and learning how the human body works always amazed me. God created us so intricately and in such a fascinating way. Our bodies are made up of many parts functioning for one purpose: to give us life. Our skeletons provide the framework and protect our internal organs. Our nerves provide a message system to our brain. Our arteries and veins keep the blood going. Our digestive system breaks down food and sends it out as energy. If one part fails, the whole system is affected. Even something as small as a broken toe can make walking difficult. This truth is why the Bible often uses the analogy of a body to describe the church.

Read Romans 12:3-8. Paul wrote this letter to the church in Rome. He wanted to remind believers that they were no longer just individuals who thought only of themselves; they were part of a family of believers. They were to function as one body, using all their individual gifts for each others' benefit and as an example of the true community that comes through Jesus Christ. The followers of Christ in Rome were part of God's global Church but lived in close community with their local body. Each member was vital to their local body and had a responsibility in seeing that they were reflecting Christ through their relationships with each other and in the way they interacted with the world.

You and I are called to see our place in our local church in the same way. When we go through each day, we need to understand that we're not doing life alone, and we were not made to live for Christ by ourselves. We're not just a part of God's global Church around the world. God created us to be a part of a local community of believers, and that community is an example of the family of Christ to the entire world. You and I have been gifted to play a specific part in our local body of believers, and it doesn't function as well unless we're all doing our part.

REFLECT

1. What does it mean for you to exist as part of a larger body?

2. Why is it so important for you to take your responsibility with your local church seriously?

3. How can you better connect with your local church and its mission in your community?

VERSE
nineteen

HOW, THEN, CAN THEY CALL ON THE ONE THEY HAVE NOT BELIEVED IN? AND HOW CAN THEY BELIEVE IN THE ONE OF WHOM THEY HAVE NOT HEARD? AND HOW CAN THEY HEAR WITHOUT SOMEONE PREACHING TO THEM?

ROMANS 10:14

Our culture knows who God is, right? I mean, just watch any number of celebrity awards shows, and you'll hear them thanking God for their success in their latest album or even their latest scandalous movie. People are constantly texting "OMG." That's definitely a reference to God. But does our culture really know who they're talking about? Do people around us really know that God holds the universe in its place, that He's in control of every breath we take, and that we were created to have a relationship with Him? How will they know the truth?

Read Romans 10:13-17. Paul spent many of the first chapters of Romans explaining salvation—everyone's need for it and how Jesus provided the way for it. Paul explained that salvation for everyone comes from God's grace through faith in Jesus Christ alone. Paul then turned his attention to the importance of sharing the great news of salvation with others. The church in Rome was to take the message of salvation to their cities and beyond. He explained that Jesus chose the Church to be His way of bringing His name to those who do not know Him—His people are His Body in the world. The main purpose as a local body of believers is to be the voice that spreads the gospel to all people.

Our mission as the Body of Christ is the same. It's our job to tell others the truth about the God whom they reference in speeches and texts but barely know. We're the voices that make Christ known to those who don't yet have a relationship with Him. When we use our gifts and abilities to help build up the Body, we become a part of working together for Christ's purpose. Our words and actions display the truth of God to the world.

REFLECT

1. How does your culture demonstrate that they don't truly know who God is?

2. If an opportunity happened for you to share the gospel, what would you say or do?

3. Ask God to put someone in your life this week whom you can share the good news of Christ with.

VERSE 20

While they were worshiping the Lord and fasting, the Holy Spirit said, "Set apart for me Barnabas and Saul for the work to which I have called them." ACTS 13:2

I love the missions conference that my church holds every year. You get to eat unique food that keeps your stomach on its toes, and you get to hear missionaries from all over the world tell exciting stories of their joys and trials. We tend to sit back and admire those people as if they were rare and special for giving their lives to make the gospel known to the ends of the earth. We're so glad that God has called them to do that. The truth is God has called everyone in the Church to the mission field in one way or another. All of us are a rare and special breed.

Read Acts 13:1-3. The church in Antioch had been actively sharing the gospel with unbelievers around their community (Acts 11:20-21). Then, while the people were praying and fasting, God called Barnabas and Saul to go out and preach the gospel beyond the borders of Antioch. Although not every person in the Antioch church was called to go with Barnabas and Saul, they were a part of the mission by praying and sending these missionaries. The church is not simply called to spread the gospel in a local community but all over the world. The church at Antioch was obedient to this call.

The mission of our churches has not changed. We're called to take the gospel to the world. God's call will look different in each of our lives, but we should all find a way to be involved in local and global missions. Praying, giving, and going are all ways to be involved and obedient to God's call. The possibilities for spreading the gospel around the world are endless. It's our call as the Church and our local body. So get involved. You're a missionary too.

REFLECT

1. Does God call churches (local bodies) to choose between local and global missions?

2. What comes to mind when you think of missionaries?

3. How do you feel when you think of yourself as a missionary?

4. How will you be involved in the Church's mission to take the gospel outside your local church walls — locally and globally?

VERSE 21

> RELIGION THAT GOD OUR FATHER ACCEPTS AS PURE AND FAULTLESS IS THIS: TO LOOK AFTER ORPHANS AND WIDOWS IN THEIR DISTRESS AND TO KEEP ONESELF FROM BEING POLLUTED BY THE WORLD.
>
> JAMES 1:27

On January 12, 2010, Haiti suffered a devastating earthquake. Experts estimate that 200,000 people were killed and 1.5 million became homeless that day. Believers began to give their time and resources for people who were hungry and dying of dehydration and lack of medical care. But did you know that prior to that disaster Haiti was the poorest country in the western hemisphere? People had already been dying of dehydration; there were already orphaned children; medical care was almost non-existent. Why did it take a natural disaster to set our eyes on this desperate place?

Read James 1:27. James was addressing an issue in several churches in which some people had become focused on pursuing worldly riches and were neglecting to put their faith into action. James wanted the people of these early churches to know what faith in action really looked like. They were not supposed to be focused on things that don't last but rather on meeting the needs of others who could not take care of themselves. If they were truly people who had given their lives to Christ, then loving others and practically caring for others' needs would be an outpouring of their faith.

There's tremendous spiritual need around the world, and we cannot neglect God's command to put our faith into action by being His Church for people who need to see Him. God calls the local body to care for the most vulnerable people. We don't do this so that we can check off a box, earn a badge, or feel good about ourselves. We're commanded by God to care for people, and when we do, the world can see the genuine faith of His Church. It's our responsibility to love and care for those around us. Every day.

REFLECT

1. Why is it so easy to ignore all the great needs around you?

2. How should your faith affect the way that you interact with the world around you?

3. What are some needs in your church, community, and the world? What can you do today to help meet some of those needs?

VERSE 22

So that you may become blameless and pure, children of God without fault in a crooked and depraved generation, in which you shine like stars in the universe.
PHILIPPIANS 2:15

What if you found out today that God didn't exist and that being a Christ-follower was meaningless? How would your life change? I imagine it would be drastically different, right? You have shaped the desires of your heart and the way you spend your time and energy on Christ and His will for your life. Or have you? It would be as if a glaring star in a dark sky just went black. Or would it? Everyone would notice how much your life would have to readjust to this startling new discovery. Or would they? You would have to completely rebuild. Or would you?

Read Philippians 2:14-15. Paul explained to the believers at Philippi that they were to be blameless and pure in the way they lived. They weren't to do this merely for their own benefit but so that the world around them would see God. They lived in a world full of crooked and depraved people who looked merely to their own interests. The people in the Philippian church were supposed to shine like stars in their dark world through the way they conducted their lives. As a result, the world would be able to see the character of God and hopefully come to worship Him.

Humanity hasn't changed since the time of the early Philippian church. People are still crooked and self-centered. We, as God's people, are to have lives that look so starkly different from this world that we look like a flashlight in the middle of a dark house. This means that we'll stick out—we won't be normal. The church is supposed to look different. Christ makes a difference in our lives, and we should reflect that to the world. Is your life a bright star, or do you blend into a dark world?

REFLECT

1. How does your life look different because of Christ?

2. Why is it scary to live differently than our culture expects?

3. In what ways will you begin to make changes in your life so that you can shine brighter?

VERSE
twenty-three

BY THIS ALL MEN WILL KNOW THAT YOU ARE MY DISCIPLES, IF YOU LOVE ONE ANOTHER.

JOHN 13:35

Yes, they'll know we are Christians by our love. I sang those words at my final day of summer camp as a proud ten-year-old wearing really cool neon orange socks. I thought about that song years later when I sat in an orphanage in Russia. A little girl sat in the lap of the woman in charge. The woman rocked the girl back and forth, singing in her sweet little ear. The girl smiled as this woman so lovingly cared for her. That woman, a follower of Christ, was giving her life to love those children who had no mothers. She was demonstrating her love for Christ by her love for others.

Read John 13:34-35. Jesus gave this command during the Last Supper, where He once again told His disciples that He was about to leave them. His work on earth was almost complete, and He was going to ascend to heaven after His death and resurrection. In the gospels, Jesus repeatedly talked about loving brothers, neighbors, and even enemies. Here, He made it clear that the way His followers are to love others is by loving them in the same way that He would. They are bound to each other and are to love each other in such a way that the world would look at them and see that they are children of God.

Jesus commands our churches to interact in the same way. As brothers and sisters in Christ, we're family. We're to love each other in a profound and sacrificial way. The people outside our churches should be able to look in and see us showing grace, care, concern and unconditional love for each other. The world should be able to look at our lives and know that we're Christians by our love.

REFLECT

1. Why is love for others a true mark of a disciple of Christ?

2. Do you find it easy to love the Christ-followers around you? Why or why not?

3. How have you shown more selfishness than love to others?

4. What would it mean for you to truly love those around you in a sacrificial way?

VERSE 24

There were no needy persons among them. For from time to time those who owned lands and houses sold them, brought the money from the sales and put it at the apostles' feet, and it was distributed to anyone as he had need.
ACTS 4:34-35

I have a friend who grew up celebrating Thanksgiving a little bit differently than most people. While her friends were celebrating a feast with their relatives every year, my friend sat down to feast with strangers. You see, if her dad knew someone in the church with no place to go for Thanksgiving, he would invite him or her to come to their house to eat. In the beginning she thought of it simply as a meal for Thanksgiving outcasts, but as she sat around the table with those people year after year she began to see them for who they were—family.

Read Acts 4:32-35. This passage is about the early church in Jerusalem and how the believers took care of each other. The followers of Christ gave their resources to the apostles so that they could distribute it to the brothers and sisters around them who were in need. They cared for one another and gave to one another so that no one went hungry; no one went without shelter; and no one had needs that were not being met. What an amazing sight it would have been to see those people coming together as one, unified by Christ, and bound to one another so tightly! They truly were family.

The early followers of Christ are an example to us of how we are to interact with our brothers and sisters in Christ. Our churches are to be a place where we come together and care for the needs of fellow believers around us and around the world. When we love each other this way, the world sees the love of Christ in our churches. Our church family is not in competition to see who can get the biggest and best stuff for a comfortable life. We are believers who love sacrificially because we take care of our family.

REFLECT

1. How did the early Christ-followers show Christ to the world by caring for one another?

2. Why is it important for us to be aware of the needs of the people in our community of Christ-followers?

3. What types of needs can you be involved in helping to meet? What can you do this week to help take care of your fellow believers?

VERSE 25

IT WAS HE WHO GAVE SOME TO BE APOSTLES, SOME TO BE PROPHETS, SOME TO BE EVANGELISTS, AND SOME TO BE PASTORS AND TEACHERS, TO PREPARE GOD'S PEOPLE FOR WORKS OF SERVICE, SO THAT THE BODY OF CHRIST MAY BE BUILT UP.

EPHESIANS 4:11-12

Ah, the pizza wedge. It's a stance that snow skiing instructors use for new skiers. You form it by turning the tops of your skis close together so that they form the shape of a pizza wedge with your skis. It's awkward, but it works. As you improve, instructors teach you to float beautifully down the hill with the more dignified side-to-side approach. But imagine what it would be like if there were no guidance. What if they just gave a thumbs-up and pushed you down the hill? It would be no time before you were tending to your many wounds. Most of the time we just need instruction to be able to do things successfully.

Read Ephesians 4:11-16. Paul focused his attention on the leaders of the church at Ephesus in this passage. He wanted to make sure that they knew their spiritual gifts were for the purpose of the church body. They were supposed to use their gifts to build up the people in their church so that those believers could grow in spiritual maturity and be prepared for works of service as a part of the mission of Christ. God had called all of His followers at Ephesus to be a part of His mission, and the church was to be a part of equipping their members to be used by Him for His purposes.

Our churches are no different. The local church must be about helping to develop gifts so that the whole body can go and be a part of God's work. The church should be a community where we're helping each other find our place in God's mission. We weren't created to point our skis down the hill and hope it goes well. God gave us community to help us as we learn to navigate through this life.

REFLECT

1. Do you consider your local church a place where you can become equipped to serve God?

2. How do you seek to become an active participant in ministry instead of leaving it for the church staff or other leaders?

3. What are you actively doing to grow spiritually and become equipped for God's mission?

4. How can you be a part of equipping others and helping them grow spiritually?

VERSE 26

And the things you have heard me say in the presence of many witnesses entrust to reliable men who will also be qualified to teach others. 2 TIMOTHY 2:2

A long time ago, somebody thought it would be really funny to ask, "Why did the chicken cross the road?" Then somebody answered, "Why?" And the first person replied, "To get to the other side." After they cried laughing, they proceeded to tell the joke to all their friends, who then told their friends, who told all their friends who—well, you get the idea. It's crazy how fast something can spread. If you don't think so, just wait for the next YouTube forward.

Read 2 Timothy 2:1-2. Paul wrote this letter while he was in prison in Rome. He knew that he would likely be killed soon because of his faith. Paul encouraged Timothy to teach faithful men and women the truths about Jesus so that they, in turn, could spread the same truths to other faithful men and women. This kind of teaching is the picture of intentional discipleship in the local church and the fulfillment of the Great Commission. Discipleship builds up the church toward spiritual maturity so that each member is growing and investing in others. The spread of the gospel would essentially stop if the community left discipleship up to a select few leaders. Paul was clear that the line of discipleship continues with all Christ-followers.

Spreading the truth about God's Word from one teacher to another did the job then, and it continues to be the model for our churches today. Are we as believers actively involved in training others to spread the truth of the gospel all over our communities? If we haven't been, then we're missing out on a key part of being Christ-followers. Let's decide today that we're going to spread the truth of God's Word to a few, so that they can do the same, so that—well, you get the idea!

REFLECT

1. Why is the cycle of discipleship so important in the spiritual growth and maturity of Christ-followers?

2. How do you see your church living out Paul's instructions to Timothy?

3. How has someone invested in your spiritual growth?

4. List a few people of the same gender that you could teach about the truth of the gospel. If you don't know anyone, then ask God to put someone in your life that you can share with.

VERSE
twenty-seven

NOW THE BEREANS WERE OF MORE NOBLE CHARACTER THAN THE THESSALONIANS, FOR THEY RECEIVED THE MESSAGE WITH GREAT EAGERNESS AND EXAMINED THE SCRIPTURES EVERY DAY TO SEE IF WHAT PAUL HAD SAID WAS TRUE.

ACTS 17:11

Did you know that there is an African butterfly that can make itself invisible when it senses danger? It doesn't just change colors; it actually becomes completely transparent. The military is using the wings of that butterfly to test a new synthetic material that will be capable of completely blending in with its surroundings. They call it Project Vanishing Act.

Yep, I completely made that up. But it sounded really amazing, right? You can't believe everything you read or hear just because it sounds good or exciting. If you want to know the truth, it's your job to check it out for yourself.

Read Acts 17:11. Paul and Silas were on a missionary journey to proclaim the message of salvation found through Jesus. In an earlier visit to Thessalonica, the message of Christ didn't sit well with the Thessalonian Jews. They drove the followers of Christ out of their city. When Paul visited the Berean Jews, though, they were open to hear the gospel message. Instead of rejecting or accepting it without question, they were serious about discipleship and examined the Scriptures to determine for themselves if what Paul said was true. As a result, many of the Bereans trusted in the truth of Christ and became believers.

If the church body is not careful, we can get lazy in our study and accept anything as truth, even a vanishing butterfly. We can take a message we've heard and throw it out because we don't like what was said, or we can also put great worth in a message because it makes us feel good. God's Word is our authority, and everything we hear must be in line with His Word. It's our job, as God's church, to know His Word and test everything we hear against it.

REFLECT

1. What was the difference between the Thessalonians' religion and the Bereans' desire to follow God in this passage?

2. Why is it so important for God's Word to be authoritative in your life?

3. What priority is God's Word in your life?

4. Make a habit of hiding God's Word in your heart. Start by memorizing the verse that you read today, and then keep reading and memorizing God's Word throughout the week.

VERSE 28

If your brother sins against you, go and show him his fault, just between the two of you. If he listens to you, you have won your brother over. MATTHEW 18:15

"So did you hear that Chris and his girlfriend had to sit down with Chris' parents last night? Apparently they found some seriously inappropriate text messages the two had been sending each other. Don't tell anyone I told you. I just thought you should know so you could pray for him. He needs it." Ever been part of a conversation like that? That's what we like to call gossip, masked in the pseudo-caring language of "Christian-eze." Though we often get it wrong, there's a right way to approach a brother or sister who's struggling with sin.

Read Matthew 18:15-17. In this passage, Jesus addressed how the local church should deal with sin among brothers and sisters. Jesus said that addressing sickness in one part of the body is crucial in order for the whole body to function as it's supposed to. He told His disciples that if their brother or sister were sinning, they were to go to that person alone and lovingly confront that person's sin. If that approach didn't work, then an increasing number of people would get involved. If, during this process, the one who had sinned repented, then that person would once again function to their fullest potential, and the Body of Christ would be stronger because of it.

It's important for us to address sins that we see in each other so that we can keep the whole body healthy. Be careful that you see how He told us to do this, though. Gossip and careless words should play no part in it. It's not everyone's business. Involve as few people as possible. You should come to them as Christ always came to sinners: with unconditional love and truth. Be an example to others of how Christ would lovingly confront sin.

REFLECT

1. Why is it easy to have a fascination with other people's sin? What should your attitude be toward sin?

2. Why is it so important for you to be willing to confront others when you need to?

3. What are the dangers in confronting your brother or sister about their sin? How will you make sure that you do it in a loving way, as Christ did?

4. Who in your life can help you be accountable for unrepentant sin?

VERSE 29

> THEREFORE CONFESS YOUR SINS TO EACH OTHER AND PRAY FOR EACH OTHER SO THAT YOU MAY BE HEALED. THE PRAYER OF A RIGHTEOUS MAN IS POWERFUL AND EFFECTIVE.
>
> JAMES 5:16

We've all been actors. We've pretended to be a good daughter or son, while rolling our eyes the second our parents turn away. We've pretended to be a good friend, while being secretly jealous and manipulative. Worst of all, we've pretended to be a good Christ-follower at church, while knowing that we've sinned the minute before we walked in the church doors. God knows you're not perfect, and that's why He sent His Son. Your job is to be honest, and the second you are, you begin to experience true community.

Read James 5:16. James told the church that if they were to truly function as the Body of Christ, they must confess their sins and pray for each other. They needed to be open and honest with each other about their struggles and their brokenness so that true healing and community could take place. They didn't need to be afraid to be open about their sin because the community of believers would love them unconditionally as they asked God for forgiveness. Through this transparency, the church would know how to pray for each other's needs, and their prayers would be powerful and effective.

Honesty and accountability are vital to community. If we want to be a church that the world sees as the Body of Christ, then we must be open with each other and pray fervently for each other. When a person who's surrendered to Jesus Christ—and who's under the direction and guidance of the Holy Spirit—prays for another person, that prayer will be highly effective. Confession and prayer are vital to the life of our churches, and it begins with you and me. We need to stop being actors and let the world see how the living Christ affects our lives and how we care for each other.

REFLECT

1. Why is honesty and confession within the community so important?

2. Do you feel as if you can be honest about sin in your life with the Christ-followers who are close to you? Why or why not?

3. Why is being transparent with others so difficult? Why do we want to portray ourselves as having it all together?

4. Who can you pray for in your life that's struggling with sin right now?

VERSE 30

Brothers, if someone is caught in a sin, you who are spiritual should restore him gently. But watch yourself, or you also may be tempted. GALATIANS 6:1

Otis was the first dog that was ever in my life. He chewed off the head of my doll, but I forgave him. He really was an amazing dog. Once, some family friends asked if their dog could come over and hang with Otis. They thought that Otis' obedience was sure to rub off. So Patches came, and we discovered through much chewing and digging that it was much easier for Patches to influence Otis than the other way around. Doing the right thing always seems to be harder when there's temptation around.

Read Galatians 6:1-2. Paul knew that the church in Galatia was made up of people, and people are sinners. Each person struggled with sin and needed help. Paul told the Galatians that they should come alongside their brothers and sisters who were struggling with sin so that they could help restore each other in their relationship with God. Paul warned the Galatians that they shouldn't be overly confident when helping someone because they could easily become tempted with the same sin. They were to approach the situation with humility and reliance upon God.

In our community of believers, we should be helping each other as we struggle with sin. We should not only be praying for each other, but we should be walking through the fire with each other and holding each other up as we break the cycles of sin in our lives. It's so important for us to be reading God's Word daily and praying that God will keep us clean. We've got to be careful if we're going to try to help those around us who are struggling. It's much easier than we might think to go from being the positive influence to the one trapped in sin.

REFLECT

1. Why is it difficult to help your brother or sister who is stuck in a certain type of sin instead of just talking about them?

2. How does caring for each other when we're struggling help to strengthen the Body of Christ?

3. What measures can you take to ensure that your way is kept pure and that you continue to walk blamelessly?

4. Identify some challenging temptations in your life that you can ask someone to help you guard against.

VERSE
thirty-one

LET US NOT GIVE UP ON MEETING TOGETHER, AS SOME ARE IN THE HABIT OF DOING, BUT LET US ENCOURAGE ONE ANOTHER—AND ALL THE MORE AS YOU SEE THE DAY APPROACHING.

HEBREWS 10:25

I recently had coffee with my friend Allison. She told me she's taking a break from church. She hasn't given up on Jesus, just on some of His followers. "The church is either too judgmental or they're fake," she explained. "Some of them won't reach out to their culture, and some of them are trying way too hard to be cool. They don't care about humanitarian issues the way they should. They need to learn the true meaning of love. I'm just going to do this Jesus thing on my own for a while and see how it works out. I give up."

Read Hebrews 10:24-25. The writer of Hebrews was telling the early Church to never give up. He explained to those believers that the local church was vital because it provided community and encouragement in a time that was evil and would only get worse. If they were in need, if they were discouraged, if they were being tempted or were straying, the church would be the hands and feet of Christ to those believers. And not only was the local church beneficial to spiritual growth, it was actually the means through which the gospel would be spread to the world!

As we've read over and over these past 31 days, God created you and me for community. Starting with Genesis, God has been setting up the Church to carry out His purpose. Now, as you and I live as Christ-followers, we're commanded to be a part of God's Church. If we're believers, then we must rely on God to lead us to a local church who's a part of His mission. This community will encourage and care for us in this life and help us fulfill God's mission in this world. Don't give up!

REFLECT

1. Why is it sometimes tempting to walk away from the church and try to walk through the life of a Christ-follower on your own?

2. How will you commit to invest in your local church?

3. Take a minute to commit before God to always be a part of His local church and to caring for His people.

closing

Hey! You made it to the end! It's like making it to the maps at the end of your Bible.

Hopefully by now you realize that you're part of something much larger than yourself. You're part of a huge family that includes even the islands of Tonga. You play a vital role in this family, even now. We can easily think that we have to wait until we're older to make a difference in our church. We also can easily think that we don't have responsibility in the church until we're older. Both of these thoughts are not true. God has called you to be His representative in the world now. No matter what you do, you're living as His active Church in the world. Make it count!

Being God's Church in the world means that you'll look different from everyone else—your life will be one that reflects God and doesn't conform to our culture, no matter how difficult that may be. Being His Church also means that you will see differently from everyone else—what matters to God will matter to you. In this life as God's Church, persecution will come, but remember that only a life that honors Christ and helps others do the same matters in the end.

Our prayer is that after studying God's Word with the help of this book, you're experiencing the benefits of spending time in prayer and Scripture and letting God's Spirit conform you more into the image of Christ each day through His Word.

Be the Church.

ABOUT THE AUTHOR

EMILY DARNELL HOOTEN is a follower of Jesus Christ and a firm believer in the love, hope, honesty, grace, and life change that come through truly knowing Him. That's why she believed so much in writing this book . . . and also because she really likes teenagers. She's a graduate of Samford University, has worked on summer staff as a seminar leader at a youth camp, and has been on staff with two different church student ministries. Emily lives in Birmingham, Alabama with her singing husband Chuck and is a proud mommy to Lily and Ava. Emily also loves stars, sour straws, her dog Ruby, laughing, taking pictures, and she would love the chance to meet some of you one day.

EXECUTIVE EDITORS
Jeremy Maxfield
Jenny Riddle

COPY EDITOR
Lynn Groom

CONTRIBUTING EDITOR
Andy Blanks

GRAPHIC DESIGN
Katie Beth Shirley

ART DIRECTOR
Drow Francis

PUBLISHING ASSISTANTS
Lee Moore
Janie Walters

STILL THIRSTY FOR GOD'S WORD?

If you liked this DEVOTIONAL JOURNAL, check out our OTHER TITLES.

- 60+ visually appealing pages
- short, relevant daily devotions
- guided questions for journaling
- easy read for teens
- suggested usage plans
- great add-on to a just**like**christ study

AND MORE AT
31VERSES.COM